365

a year of writing adventures

Daily Prompts
& sample poems

by

Carol Willette Bachofner, MFA

365, a year of writing adventures

ISBN # 9780359557790   First Edition

ACKNOWLEDGEMENTS

Thanks to Virginia Weare Parsons, BH Fairchild, and Jack Myers who believed in me and helped me to understand the power of words. To Richard Wilbur whose example of writing discipline and ethics keep me going day after day.

As always, to Bill who encourages me and reads everything.

PUBLISHER: Such a Girl Press

Cover art: photograph by the author
Author Photo: Bill Bachofner

Design & Formatting: Inked Toad Press

Printed in the USA
$16.95 US
$21.34 CAN

For online orders: www.carolbachofner.com (Books & Media)
To set up a writing workshop (groups of 6 or more) contact: mainepoet@me.com

365

a year of writing adventures

Daily Writing Prompts
(with sample poems)

created by

Carol Willette Bachofner

Table of Contents

365: a year of writing adventures

Prologue:

Instructions For Using This Book

In these pages are daily writing prompts, designed by me for my own poetic practice, as part of a 365 discipline in poetry undertaken in November 2012.

The prompts are set forth here for any writer of poems **(or any writer at all)** who wants to take up the challenge to practice the art by way of prompts, a week at a time, a month at a time, or for the whole year. The prompts are arranged as the author worked on them, by month and by week.

Each month's prompts are preceded by a short note of encouragement and inspiration, as well as a sample from my own writing discipline.

Go on, try these. Don't cheat now...just begin by following the prompts as they come.

When you encounter some of the prompts, you may scratch your head and say, *what? how am I going to write about THAT?*

Don't fret; just do it.

NOTE for writers of essays or short stories:

These prompts are easily adaptable for you! Wherever it says "poem" in the instructions, think essay or story as well. In case of a question on any of the prompts that seem geared for poets, you can contact me via my website to get an alternate prompt or a way to use that prompt for something other than a poem.

November

When responding/writing to a prompt, or a series of prompts, it is helpful to take a few notes on what your first impression is when you read the prompt for the first time. There is no need to over-think here. Just scribble away in a free-write mode, ranging as far and wide as your mind takes you.

When you have completed your free-write, read the prompt again and begin with a first line. Remember, each poem is a spontaneous DRAFT. You can and will revise later.

Here is an example from my own November challenge (#13):

Moet and Chandon

She's a killer, queen
of every situation, like a bee
hovering so close to the males
they vibrate with her winged
attention. She needs nothing
more than their lives, and nectar
to make her fat and fecund.
It's Moet and Chandon, snappy
choice in her crystal flute, held
with manicured hands, fine rings
on fingers just slim enough to fit
through the belt loops
of the handsome men who court her.
She's the Marie Antoinette of her day,
a thousand mirrors catch her every move,
but not so close as to show her flaws:
she's a killer queen, a femme fatale,
a spider webbed widow with a plan.

— written while listening to *Killer Queen*, by Queen

November, Week One

1. Write a *small stone** poem focus on some small thing and write about it.
2. Find and use four words from a book — I used a dedication in a book.
3. Write about an object nearby.
4. Write a poem, inspired by or dedicated to a lost loved one.
5. Write in response to a random page of poetry by someone else.
6. Write a political poem; don't hold back. Can be from current politics or historical politics.
7. Ten Questions/Ten Answers poem; pose 10 questions, then answer in a poem. Adapt for essay by posing the questions and answering in a short essay.

November, Week Two

8. Write a nature poem. Get all Rachel Carson about this!
9. Write about something that fills a need.
10. Write a love or an anti-love poem.
11. Write about a specific location important to you (can be any place).
12. Write about a beverage. Make it about a person too.
13. Write while listening to music. Include some lyrics
14. Write a somewhat erotic poem using pork… look up the Hoggala form.

November, Week Three

15. Write in an "invented" form... invent and write!

16. Write a shopping poem, pro or con.

17. Write a job poem. Can be a rant if you like.

18. Write today's poem about the passage of time.

19. Write a "green" poem, your interpretation of "green."

20. Make today's poem a gratitude piece.

21. Write a family recipe poem.

November, Week Four

22. Write about a person in your family and something that happened to that person. but don't let the piece drip with drama.

23. Write a poem about housework and a special occasion.

24. Story poem is today's challenge. How about a nice *once upon a time?*

25. Write today's poem, using 4-5 words from a famous poem. I chose to use a Millay poem for my words, four of her words start

26. Write from your body; make it as if your body is something else.

27. Write a horoscope poem (find your horoscope, write in response to that).

28. Use one of the following phrases in today's poem: *It's no place I really know, or it's every place I've ever known*

November. Week Five

29. Write about a lost pet, an homage or a lament.
30. Write about something ending, a finality.

December

When responding to a prompt, there is the tendency to spend TOO LITTLE time on the details in favor of being spontaneous. But it is a balance. Consider making a list of active verbs and concrete nouns when you have finished your free-write. These will be the pillars of your poem/draft and lead you to a solid revision later.

Here is a sample poem, taken from my December prompt responses (#7)

Nepenthe*
  — a widow's lament

She might have taken something strong
for the sorrow that wrapped her
as she lay sleeping, but here she is
waking without you and lying
in a bed of tears. The ancient Greeks
knew medicine for all things: strange
salves to rub away warts, potions to cure
all manner of illness, but they really knew
sorrow, tragedy being the main act
of every play. She wants nepenthe
stirred or swirled into her cocoa
before spending another night alone.
You never liked taking even an aspirin,
would endure painful teeth or a blown
knee until she insisted you do something.
You thought pain a badge of honor.
She has in mind a certain ancient
formula, an oblivion of sorrow.

* a medicine for sorrow, "drug of forgetfulness" mentioned in ancient Greek literature. Nepenthe was a potion used by the ancients to induce forgetfulness of pain or sorrow, a potion capable of causing oblivion of grief or suffering, an avoidance of grieving.

December, Week One

1. Write a poem about sudden, inclement weather.
2. Write about a school experience.
3. Write about a piece of family furniture.
4. Write about something "gained."
5. Write a haiku about a drink. Look up haiku form if you need to do so.
6. Write about something saved.
7. Write about a poison.

December, Week Two

8. Write a poem about what is just outside your door or window today.

9. Use 4 words from a book you have read recently. Open the book to page 9 and find the words there.

10. Write about an incident/memory from childhood.

11. Write a poem about a long-ago love.

12. Write about an item of clothing or jewelry.

13. Write a poem about a deal or bargain you made or would make.

14. What is left behind as winter arrives? Write about missing it, or about being glad it's gone.

December, Week Three

15. Write a poem inspired by the phrase, *in the front row*

16. Find a family photo (from a while back) and write about one of the people in the photo who seems different from everyone else.

17. Write a poem of opposites.

18. Write a triolet or a double or triple triolet (look up the form if you need to)

19. Write about a fight.

20. Write about a piece of mail.

21. Listen to a song from long ago and write from a snippet.

December, Week Four

22. Choose a lesser holiday (or one from another culture) and ask yourself 4 questions about it. Then write a poem from your answers.

23. Write about change, using these words: *sleep, stones, fury, careful.*

24. Write a poem from the perspective of the first minutes after waking or the last minutes before falling asleep.

25. Write a seasonal poem of despair or sorrow.

26. New house, new city, new job.... write about newness or change.

27. Use the starter, *I catch up with you.*

28. In a library book you've just checked out is an envelope... what is in there? Write a poem about surprising news.

December, Week Five

29. Name a river. Write about it.

30. Write a poem that is a premonition or warning.

31. This is your final poem of the discipline! Poet's choice.

January

So, let's get started. Don't worry that you will do something "wrong" or "mess it up." The plan is simple. The big thing is (of course) to get writing and keep going with it through the whole 365 days of our discipline. After all, a discipline is a plan that builds a work ethic, a habit, a way of being. So, jump in and begin.
I admit that when I started, I wondered whether I would last the month. (I began my discipline in November as part of a *NaNoWriMo* …National November Write Month). I was not at all sure I had the staying power or self-discipline. I have always been a "fits and starts" kind of person in many ways. But when the first month was at its end, I wanted to go on. I had built a habit. You can too. And maybe at the end of a month or two you will fade off and not do every single day. But you will have a prompt for every day, a way IN. So, go… write.

Here is a sample poem from my January discipline (# 25)

Losses
Stand in the street, woman
whose children sleep
in the back seat of her car, hidden
from view behind the abandoned factory.
Stand in a doorway, out of the chill wind
that bristles leaves fiercely held
by the trees. Wait until school is out.
In your bag, dinner for three rescued
from the grocery dumpster. Stand
in the snow that begins again for the third
day in a row, watch for someone to drop
a glove, or leave a scarf on the bench.
Stand in the street all day. Stand while
people pass you by, sneers on their faces,
not knowing you used to stand by a warm stove,
stirring soup you made for your kids. Stand.

January, Week One

1. First poem of the year: write about a decision

2. Use this phrase *think of the fish* somewhere in today's poem.

3. Write about a task you avoid.

4. Write about an unusual relative.

5. Write about something hidden (get this from an item in current events)

6. You have to give away 1/2 of your possessions. Write about this.

7. Write a limerick (or write about wisdom gone wrong)

January, Week Two

8. The poem today is trip "down the rabbit hole." Write a lune or a lune sequence. (look up this form online)

9. You have a superpower. What is it and will you use it for good or evil?

10. Write a poem using a line or phrase from another poem.

11. What is your favorite room of the house? Write about the room or part of the room.

12. Write about a pencil or pen.

13. Write a magical poem about an unusual thing to be found in an icicle.

14. Write about yourself as part of a literary (or famous) family.

January, Week Three

15. Write about a time when you were "naughty."

16. Use these words: algid, tepid, burning, frozen and write a poem about a relationship.

17. Write a poem about a specific bird.

18. What is your fear? Write your way out of it.

19. Write about an inheritance (something you received, will receive, or will leave to someone when you die).

20. Something is growing.... what is it?

21. If you are female, write as a male; if you are male, write as a female (persona poem).

January, Week Four

22. Commit a RAP (Random Act of Poetry) by delivering one of the previous poems somewhere unusual for poetry to be; then write today's poem about the delivery.

23. Use a phrase from another language and write a poem around it; use it as the title or the first line of your poem.

24. Write about you own hands.

25. Start your poem with: *stand in the street.*

26. End your poem with: *in case there were rumors.*

27. Write about a math formula.

28. Write an historic poem about a Greek or Roman myth.

January, Week Five

29. Write a sequel to a fairy tale.

30. Make up a rule and write about it. Write a fanciful poem; do NOT get serious at all.

31. Write either an *ars poetica* or an ekphrastic poem. You might go to a gallery for the latter, expanding your experience with the intertextuality of art and writing.

February

Writing daily poems is a good way to keep track of yourself. In responding to prompts, you are given a chance to step out of or aside from the daily grind of your regular life. This shorter month gives you some breathing room.

Here is a poem from my February practice (#8) wherein I am responding to some re-reading I was doing in the life of Poe. Note the literary allusions in this poem. Have you read Poe? Maybe you'll want to now:

Poorer Poe

Poe had to neglect poetry
to favor commerce, to take
care of days and nights
with their demands. Not his
desire, his search
for something deep, alive
and a-fire. His talents ran amok
into dark places, sad lanes
and purloined correspondence.

No one complains. Hardly anyone
notices these days.

But we are the poorer
for his commerce, rich enough
some say to be able to hear the Raven
speak forevermore. We sigh
for the lost Lenore and for ourselves.

February, Week One

1. Write a poem using food as a metaphor for an emotion.

2. Write about a party you were not invited to attend.

3. Use 3 weather words and a book title in today's poem.

4. Use *batoto yetu* (Swahili for "our children" and write a poem about or for children. I complicated this by using a French and a German phrase for the same.

5. Write a poem about weather; this could be physical or emotional weather.

6. Write a poem using the two phrases: *torn minds* and *mended mirrors.*

7. Write a poem about starting over on foreign soil; what would it be like to be an ex-pat?

February, Week Two

8. Write a poem using the phrase *something deep.*

9. Write a poem using *on this ordinary evening.*

10. Write an address poem.

11. Begin your poem within the hour between — and —.

12. Write a poem that is a contradiction or a series of contradictions.

13. Write a poem about how you are like a family member or parent; or how you are not.

14. Write a poem about a road not taken.

February, Week Three

15. Start or end a poem with *I'd prefer* _____ .

16. Write a sonnet, give it a shape or make it different somehow.

17. *All things born without wings.* Use this to inspire your poem today.

18. Write a poem with a ghost or spirit as part of the action.

19. Write today's poem using the phrase *upon the heads of stylish women;* write about hair.

20. Write one stanza of today's poem in a specific spot in daytime; return to the place at night and write the second stanza.

21. Write about something that is broken.

February, Week Four

22. Find an archaic or unusual word and use it in your poem today.

23. Write a sensual poem to a stranger.

24. Begin one stanza of today's poem with *paper may burn...*

25. Start your poem with *It's true that...*

26. Use the phrase *nothing of this is true* close to the end of the poem.

27. Find something in the news and write in response to that story or article.

28. A "kitchen poem." Write about something in the cupboard.

March

In any discipline, there is a period of "flagging energy." You want to stop, to quit, to declare *enough!* and do something else. But the trick of successful people is to keep on going, to understand this is *habit-building.* So keep on going.

Here is a poem sample from my March practice (#10).

The poem takes on a certain concreteness when it opens with a description of the symbol for sigma; then it takes off in another direction:

Σ

a beach umbrella chaise
bent, folded over to make shade
for the mermaid who seeks shore
and a rest from salt, which makes
her dizzy. Such a chemical
that coats her hair, frizzes it beyond curls,
that makes her voice husky
when she sings, that stays on her tongue
gives her a sore throat. Salt and brine.
She is not staying long —
only moments before she will dry
to a crinkle, end up like Lot's wife,
a statue on the sand, looking back
on where she could have been queen.

March, Week One

1. Write a birthday poem.
2. In the absence of words, write a poem about something that leaves you speechless.
3. Write about something that stings.
4. Romance of the onion: Write a poem that celebrates the onion (or garlic).
5. *Umbrellas of Cherbourg*: write about umbrellas and rain, maybe connect to a lost romance.
6. Town line, town limits: Write about what is on the edge of town.
7. Write about an historical figure, someone famous over 50 years ago.

March, Week Two

8. Write a science poem.
9. Write a poem interpreting a myth.
10. Write a poem using a Greek letter and set the poem near the sea.
11. Write a poem about an article of clothing; make the poem a pantoum.
12. Everyone's a critic. Write about a criticism you've received.
13. Write a meteor or falling star poem.
14. Write a sci-fi poem.

March, Week Three

15. Frost wrote: *the earth's the right place for love.* What do you say the earth's the place for?
16. Write about what you'd see hidden in a strange city if you were a flâneur. Pick a city you've never visited.
17. The Lake of the Dismal Swamp (Thomas Moore). Write about a lost soul.
18. Write an over-the-top political poem today.
19. Write about a breakup or a proposal.
20. Write a rhapsodic poem.
21. Write about a toy or a doll from your childhood.

March, Week Four

22. Don't say it: what ought you not say? Say it anyway!
23. Write about a dance style. Include specific moves and postures.
24. Go to a cemetery and find the oldest grave there. Write about the person in that grave.
25. I am a sharpened pencil. What does this say to you? Write.
26. Body work. Write a poem about a body part. An homage? A blessing? A curse?
27. Shakespeare in love... write a response to one of the Bard's sonnets, use a phrase from it in your poem.
28. Write about maple syrup, pine pitch, ambergris; got sap?

March, Week Five

29. Read Poe's poem, *To Annie.* Write in a similar tone. Quote a line if needed.

30. Write a poem about nothing.

31. Write a poem about what flows over you.

April

As we write, patterns of thoughts start to open to us, ways of looking at the world give us the way IN to our poems. If we are ready to accept that stray thoughts are a gift we can use in our writing, we will find ourselves getting increasingly creative and bold.
Let yourself be bolder this month than ever before.
Here is a sample poem from my April practice (#25):

Notes on Notes
I am *Eine Kleine Nachtmusik,* play
past bedtime and into moonrise,
my notes on notes that cleave time
and leave me dangling on twine
above the bed, like a dreamcatcher
with spider weaving mad music
to keep all of us safe in darkness,
to filter carnival dreams from nightmares.

I am strains of melody, running
under stars dead already — beyond
the 186,000 miles it took them
to get their light here for us to admire.
If you make note of my notes, play
them again in daylight, they have flattened
or grown too sharp for your palate,
for the smell of bacon frying
or the splash of juice in the jelly jar
your mother calls "glasses."

I am fine-honed music, or jazz or rap,
but always playing at night, in shadow.
I am not a brass band on the street
or a booming car stereo. I am steady
bars, glissando or lente. No fortissimo
will do for my score. *Eine Kleine Nacht*
a little bit of note on notes, a little *musik*
to make it worth opening your eyes, singing.

April, Week One

1. Write a poem of foolishness.

2. Write a poem where being "sensible" is the main feature.

3. Write a poem about sunshine.

4. Write a poem where rain is a main character or controlling metaphor.

5. Research an unusual flower. Write about a relative in terms of this flower.

6. Make up a new rule and write a poem about getting people to follow it.

7. Take a prior poem and cut out text, leaving the white space... see what new poem emerges; to read the original and compare. (Go to March poems, Day 15...week 2)

April, Week Two

8. Write an 8-line rhymed poem where the rhyming words are at the beginnings of the lines.

9. Write a poem about illness; write in a clinical tone, avoiding sentimental tones.

10. Write a poem with a numerical formula in it (such as $3 + 4 = 7 - 2 = 5$). Rhyme poem (or not).

11. Write a blank verse love poem. This is not a poem about you and your beloved.

12. What happens when the wind wakes you? Write a lament.

13. Write a poem about a farm animal and a picnic.

14. Write a villanelle about the sea or the wind. Include a person you do NOT particularly like.

April, Week Three

15. Write about something unexpected, may be positive or tragic.

16. Write a plea to another poet or poets.

17. Write a "true crime" poem.

18. Go on a virtual vacation to somewhere you've never been. What will you bring back with you?

19. Write a poem about hunger.

20. Use some of these words in today's poem: blown, ground, stand, pretend, human, porridge, forage, orange, lumen, wax, stacks.

21. Voyeur poem: what do you imagine you see in the window of a house you pass by in your car today? Write about it. DO NOT PEEP into someone's home!!! IMAGINE.

April, Week Four

22. Write a toll booth poem... write this as if you are the driver, or as if you are the booth worker.

23. Write a flag poem. NO sappy or forced patriotism please.

24. Write a poem where you are asleep and aware of someone else in the room with you.

25. Write an "I am" poem, using the name of your favorite movie or musical piece.

26. Use some or all of the following words: tape, bullet, quicksand, mirror, bowl, staple, wrench.

April, Week Five

27. Write an elegy. Mention the person's closest relative or a friend.

28. Write a poem in 3 rhymed couplets, or 3 haiku, or 3 lunes.

29. Write a poem in the voice of a teenager.

30. Write a poem about mushrooms. Do the research!

May

At the halfway point (or so) of the challenge/discipline, you must be feeling pretty good. It is nice to see how much more easily thoughts and images become poem drafts. WARNING: remember these are drafts, to be revised later when the flames have cooled. The Romantics knew this and stated it this way (paraphrasing here): to write when filled with an overflow of powerful emotion, then write when that has cooled and give the reader a chance to have her/his own emotional response to what you have put down. So remember the revision... maybe next year's project.

Here is a sample poem from my May practice (#3):

Profuse and Profane

There, on the side of the road,
orange plastic bags filled with litter,
litter you tossed from your cars
as you whizzed by, heading
to or fro. There they are, bright bundles
growing like weeds along the highways.
       Treasures of travel, profuse and profane
       evidence of bad manners, there they are.
Gone are the signs,
the warnings of fines and penalties
for dropping onto the byways
what you're done using. *Litterbugging*
seems okay now, so much more to worry
us these days like that text message,
the price of gas at the next exit.

       Better speed up, keep ahead of the traffic,
       find a motel with a swimming pool.

There, on the side of the road, a sign:
highway beautification
next 8 miles by the makers
of orange plastic bags.

May, Week One

1. Write about a bit of luck. Begin or end with "I've always had it…"
2. Write a poem that contains the following phrase: f*ollowing the back road.*
3. Make a poem that celebrates trash or trash pickers.
4. Make a poem that features feet or toes.
5. Write a 14-line poem that turns on itself at line 8 (this is not a sonnet).
6. Write a poem about another poet or a fiction writer, one whose work you admire.
7. Write a poem using the title of someone "royal."

May, Week Two

8. Write about an "invisible" illness.
9. Write about what is below ground.
10. Make a poem that somehow reverses its position, then returns to its original position.
11. Think of a house you visited as a child. Make up a scene there (imagined). Write the poem.
12. Write a poem about an historical piece of furniture or clothing.
13. Write a poem that declares itself to be your last poem ever.
14. Write a poem about coming back home after being long away.

May, Week Three

15. Write from the position of one of your ancestors. Make it a poem that addresses YOU — from that person.
16. Write a poem answering yesterday's poem.
17. Write a poem to someone not yet born.
18. Write a poem addressing a famous poet, long dead. Include a request.
19. Write a poem of advice to a poet you might be mentoring. Include a confession.
20. Make an apology poem. Have you made someone unhappy? Fix it in the poem.
21. Make a poem asking for an apology. Where have you been wronged? Fix it in the poem.

May, Week Four

22. When is a poem dangerous? Write about this.

23. Crowds and lonely spaces; connect the two in a poem.

24. Chairs or stools. Write a poem about these.

25. Island life is _____. Use this in a poem, but not the first line.

26. Write a poem about money. Can be a have/have not poem.

27. Write a 5-line poem. In line one mention a color (be creative); in line two a place you haven't been in a while; line three needs an article of clothing; line four needs the name of a person; line five should contain a secret. Now write the next five lines using the same directions with different details, except for the name of the person.

May, Week Five

28. Begin the poem with *it is the season of doors.*

29. End the poem with a line that contains *it was the season of forgetting.*

30. Find a photograph in a book or magazine. Pretend you are there and write.

31. Pick a little-celebrated holiday or festival. Write about it as if you are the honored guest.

June

Unmistakably, writing is hard work. It is easy to give up, or worse to become numbed to what we set out to accomplish. Doing a poem a day can lure one into either rut. On the flip side, doing a **discipline** can prevent that from happening. It is important therefore to keep reminding oneself that this is not a means to an end, not "production," but rather a way of being in one's writing life.

Here is a sample poem from my June practice (#8):

Quicksilver

Ballet shoes scuffed up fine —
toes at a patina, ribbons frayed
and shimmery. On stage she is all
anyone ever wanted, lithe
grace swooping like a bird of prey
over the hearts of every man
in the audience. In her mirror,
the swan returns to the pond
to its awkward start as someone
else's cast-off. No manner
of applause can undo the sobs that bubble
from where the dancing ends. Lace
edged handkerchief at her bodice,
monogram of her mother in one worn corner.
The music fades into a farmhouse kitchen
radio where, at the four o'clock hour,
Momma would twirl, pirouette
and hold in position, where chicken pies
cooled on the stove and the men
had not yet brought their rough music
to supper. A suitcase packed and hidden
behind the bedroom door, moon
rising in the uncurtained window.
On her dressing table,
a silver lipstick, opened for luck
at the five-minute call. Scent
of Momma and courage, like quicksilver.

June, Week One

1. Write about riding a boat somewhere.
2. Write about a cottage.
3. Write about the sounds of an island.
4. Write a poem about finches or swallows
5. Write a poem using some kind of old-fashioned appliance or furniture.
6. Write a 10-line poem, using the following phrase: *at night* or *as day breaks.*
7. Write a poem of six 4-line stanzas; poet's choice of topic.

June, Week Two

8. Write a poem using the following: ballerina, quicksilver, and kitchen.
9. Write a poem about deafness; what sounds does a deaf person feel rather than hear?
10. Write a poem about loss; use garden imagery.
11. Write about an old children's story, using the words *mint* or *tiger.*
12. Begin today's poem with *No part of this.*
13. What is your favorite number? Play with multiples of this number in today's poem.
14. Write about something iconic that has disappeared.

June, Week Three

15. Write about a time when you wanted to do something but held back.
16. Write a zoo poem. Use some kind of musical or literary allusion.
17. Today's poem wants to be a letter or a reply to a letter.
18. Turn on the news. Write today's poem about the lead story.
19. Write a poem about housework or a chore.
20. If you were in jail, sentenced to die (either innocent or guilty) what poem would you write? Write it.
21. Write about the place inside the place.

June, Week Four

22. *You can't kill a starfish in any usual way.* Write about this.
23. Write about a constellation.
24. *I found her/his/your letters ...* write using this phrase at the end of your poem.
25. *I'll trade the memory of this for ...* use this phrase in the middle of a poem about lying.
26. What do you say when there is nothing more to say? Write about this.
27. Write a poem about a train trip or about a specific train.
28. Write about an industrial accident or a factory fire (research this, use details from research).

June, Week Five

29. Write about a prism, and a prison.
30. Write about the day you were born; make up the details.

July

No giving up now. Vacation time is here, but not for poets who find a whole new set of impulses for writing. What about the quiet mornings when there isn't a schedule of activity for many people? What about a glut of noises outside the window that lets you know school is out for the summer? Bicycles and lawn mowers and birds a-chirp in the tree outside your window. Six more months of your 365 discipline. 181 days, 181 poems. Write on!

Here's a sample poem from my July practice (#15):

You Are Stardust

I see a peacock with a fiery tail

sweeping by in my garden, a comet of colors;

I see the glitter of the mollusk's trail

over blades of grass that once were stars

you longed for when day broke

the spell of night, its salmon face

beaming light. This is the history

of our lovely rock, our teeming oceans

that lie upon the shore, running away

then returning like a pensive child

rejects its toy only to miss it sore.

We're all related: snail & star,

blade of grass & peacock's tail.

It's a dialogue between mirrors.

We're shadow and man come together

after daylight when the sun is long, then goes

July, Week One

1. Write a poem of childhood; look back while being in the present.

2. Write a glosa or a variation on a glosa.

3. Write a once-upon-a-time poem.

4. *The white rose dies as easily as the red;* use this in your poem today.

5. *The sky holds centuries of clouds.* Use this in your poem today.

6. What would you die for?

7. Use the phrase *shadows in the café,* or write with this line in mind.

July, Week Two

8. Write using *with no particular harbor in mind* as part of today's poem.

9. Write using *arriving at a canvas of pure* _____ (use a color word here or a kind of paint).

10. Use *the kiss, the embrace, the problem* in today's poem.

11. Write a poem about favors.

12. Use the phrase *clobbered by angels*, and write a sacrilegious poem.

13. *The mask is the center of gravity.* Use this in today's poem.

14. The liberty bell is more than the crack. Write about liberty and license.

July, Week Three

15. Write a poem about self-image. Use the phrase, *a dialogue between mirrors* in your poem.
16. The way in is the way out. Write about a conundrum.
17. Write a poem about a shipwreck; use *the seam, the rip, the toss.*
18. *Love, I say, will become _____ when brought to the _____.* Use this in your poem today.
19. *As the hand vanishes, the child appears.* Use this in your poem today.
20. End today's poem with *the carrion artist works underground, works in darkness, is a thief.*
21. *Let a hundred flowers bloom, only one die.* Use this in your poem.

July, Week Four

22. At age, _____, she gave herself to a slavery of fashion; write about teen girls.
23. Write a poem that disguises something, like truth or love.
24. Write about an audience at a poetry reading.
25. Write a poem about finding a treasure when cleaning out a drawer or closet.
26. Write a camping poem.

July, Week Five

27. What color is Tuesday? Write a magical poem.

28. Write a poem that tells a story, mentioning a carousel or a flying horse.

29. Write a poem where you explore learning something surprising.

30. Write a poem about another an address where you once lived, but do not now.

31. Write a poem where someone goes mad.

August   -

Hundreds of days of poems. Anyone would be exasperated by now, tired of even knowing there must be a poem today. However, I am not done in by this. What has happened, a strange phenomenon truly, is that I am more invested than when I started. I eagerly await what prompt I will see, how I will gnaw away at it until ideas come, how I will twist it and stretch it until it's need to be on the page is urgent.

This is not a bad way for a writer of any genre to awaken. Not bad at all. It becomes more than a discipline. It becomes a returning migration to words and form, to ideas and encounters. So write and keep writing.

Sample poem from my August practice (#12):

Castings

As if the forest were alive,
as if it could stop breathing
and still live. On the floor debris
from what we do, castings
from worms we've become.

August, Week One

1. Write an address to a person you find in the phone book. Base your info solely upon what the name seems like to you.

2. Write an homage to some daily or menial task you do, give it a new look and make it special.

3. Write about doors.

4. Write about your name (choose first, middle, or last); explore the name and your feelings about it.

5. Use the following words and write a poem about a break-up: *raspberry, rain, shoes, children.*

6. Write about a piece of art that is strange to you. Be detailed, make metaphor.

7. Write about a skill you don't possess; be kind to yourself or be mean.

August, Week Two

8. Write about a clock, but don't make the poem about time.

9. You are driving through a region of the country that is unfamiliar...
what do you see? Research for accuracy. Then make it unreal,
mythical, fictional.

10. Write about virginity and gardening.

11. Discover a person in a news story and write a persona poem from
that person's "incident" or information. Can be funny or tragic, easy-
going or dangerous.

12. Write about what exists on a forest floor.

13. Include *smarting from the last time* in the poem.

14. What do you fear the most? dogs? fireworks? your head under
water? Write this.

August, Week Three

15. What one day (night) would you change? Write it.

16. Use some of the following words in today's poem: *funicular, funnel cloud, ferry, flirt, fiery.*

17. Open the dictionary to the "K" section, choose a word at random and build your poem.

18. You met someone famous in an elevator, or at a coffee shop... who? What was the conversation like? Do NOT make this about celebrity-worship.

19. The projector whirs like a tiny time machine... you step into the light. Where are you? Where is God?

20. Write about air. This is NOT a nature poem.

21. Write using a foreign phrase, preferably one that is in use somewhere currently, an idiom might be good here.

August, Week Four

22. I'm not going to _____; write about a missed travel opportunity.

23. Find a family photograph from a long time ago; choose a person who is unknown to you and write an address poem to him/her.

24. Use the following words in today's poem:
    perfumed, braid, reputation, manner, beach glass.

25. Write an ekphrastic poem; go to a gallery or museum for this.

26. Find yourself in another person's house; you are a ghost. What do you see there?

27. Write a poem based on a cliché. Really overdo the clichés.

28. Write a poem about what happens in the night while you sleep: maybe title it *Midnight Opportunities.*

August, Week Five

29. Write about riding the bus. Use the following words: *clatter, bridge, earphones, plastic, martyr, stone, feral.*

30. Write about reputation.

31. Write a poem that mixes children's stories.

September

Leaves are turning brilliant colors. I ask myself: *Am I turning dull?* It's hard to sustain any kind of long-term project, but this is not just a project; it's a discipline. As I near the finish (I cannot bear to use the "e-word") of this year in poetry, I look forward to being able to plug in when I am inspired and find poems waiting for me. September first marks the 212th day/poem. Onward toward new ideas and new horizons.

Sample Poem From my Practice (#6):

Ghosts at the Hotel

The maid cannot scrub the place
of lovers and their secrets.
Ghosts of other lovers
watch from the ceiling, the drapes,
the half-open door of the bath.
For them, it's like a movie,
a flickering on the TV screen
as night comes to its end.

They sigh, glance at one another,
wondering what that ache is
she whispers about as you dress
to leave her, the scent of her on you,
lingering and dangerous.

You cannot make them look away,
no matter if you keep the sheets
tight to your necks, the music
of yourselves muted and low.

September, Week One

1. Go to your local coffee house; eavesdrop; write from an overheard conversation.
2. Write a "mother" poem, loose interpretation ok here.
3. Write a "school" poem.
4. Write a poem about pavement. Use the following words (or not): *embed, paint, river, high heels, yellow.*
5. Write a poem that includes the following words: *spray, film, frame, camera, material, oars.*
6. Write about hotels; make it about hotel bedrooms.
7. Write the other half of yesterday's hotel poem; make it about the lobby, dining, or other common room.

September, Week Two

8. Write a poem about two "common miracles."
9. Write about animal behavior that mimics human behavior or visa versa.
10. Is your idea of paradise some PLACE or an altered state? Write about paradise.
11. What do you see in the rearview mirror? Write about regret.
12. Write a poem of warning.
13. Write about remodeling a room. Use at least three of the following words: *wreck(age), furrow, high, service, underwear, hat, scream.*
14. Write about kissing. This is NOT a romantic poem.

September, Week Three

15. Write about visitors.
16. Go to a retail store and find the most expensive item you'd love to buy. Write about penny-pinching.
17. Write a poem about travel.
18. Write a poem that celebrates sound or its absence.
19. What happens just before dawn? Write about it and use at least 4 of these words: *fulsome, planet, fold, storm, Bible, slip, horn, crease.*
20. Write a poem that is a dialogue between your younger self and your older self. NOT the now self.
21. Write a poem about pieces.

September, Week Four

22. Write a poem about a roof or a ceiling. This should be a poem of captivity.
23. Write about a nighttime activity that is unexpected.
24. What is left on the plate when a sumptuous meal is done? Write about this.
25. A stranger asks if you are _____ (the name of a person). You are tempted to say you are. Write about an encounter with a stranger.
26. Write a poem about laughter. Serious poem please.

September, Week Five

27. Write about your fingerprints.

28. Write about fire; what is gained by burning?

29. Write about getting a tattoo. Do not become literal here!

30. What strange item shows up on your x-ray?

October

October, and I find that I am not "out of gas" to continue writing daily poems. I have had surges and slumps along the way, but as I have found, the lure of a new poem is always stronger than a slump. When you find yourself thinking you cannot possible write again, the prompts (and others you may find) will inspire you to go for "just one more" poem or free-write. It's my belief that there are as many possible writing experiences as there are words in the thickest dictionary. Think about that for a minute. Now write.

Example from my discipline (#11)

The Fox

hidden in the gulley brush
at the end of our street
comes to my porch
for a rest. It's the mother
with her flame tail
at attention that calls me
from my safe window.
Her kits are denned nearby.
I hear them mewling.
She is hungry; they are too.

My cupboards yield nothing
much for foxes, some leftover
panko, figs, bread and butter
pickles we made two years ago.
She must want chicken
(a common story: foxes in the henhouse)
but it's a bit frozen still, thawing
for my dinner. She catches my eye.
Her kits call to her again.
We are mothers.
I put the chicken on the porch.

October, Week One

1. Write a poem that looks at two loves; smoosh here.

2. Write a poem that celebrates something not usually celebrated.

3. Today is the birthday of a previous lover or beau. Write a tribute to him/her and mention a specific "something" that is to be treasured in memory.

4. You are suddenly without power. Write about how dark dark is, celebrate the darkness.

5. Write about one or more philosophers, celebrating or exploring the theory(ies) or the persons.

6. Write about what you hear when it is quiet.

7. Write a poem that celebrates a body part. Use some or all of these words: *joint, pose, skin, hobble, feed, maroon, bottle*

October, Week Two

8. Write a "best day" poem; dig deep to find a memory.

9. Write about an epiphany. Use as many "surprise words" as you can without being "cute" or predictable.

10. Read something in the news or online; it should be something you don't hear about regularly; now write about it.

11. Write about an animal that shows up in your yard. Why is it there? What do you do? Make the poem about a common bond you hadn't thought of before.

12. Think of a person who has hurt or disappointed you. Write a poem praising that person.

13. Write a poem celebrating a stage of life. This is NOT a poem about you.

14. Write about a missed opportunity as if you had not missed it.

47

October, Week Three

15. Write your own obituary, in verse. Or an epitaph.

16. Write about the Periodic Table of Elements.

17. You've come down with a cold. Write a "remedy" poem.

18. Write about a childhood friend. Hero? Villain? Victim?

19. Write a poem of expectation/anticipation.

20. Write a poem that uses variations on the word "leaves, leaf." Mix it up and use past present future form of leave; include the word used as a noun/as nouns.

21. Consider what is forbidden.

October, Week Four

22. Celebrate sleeping. Write about the pleasure of a nap.

23. Write a poem using the following words: *tomorrow, yesterday, next, follow, stupefy, thyme, grease.*

24. Write a birth poem. May be from the POV of the baby, mother, midwife.

25. Write a poem about a telephone or telephoning.

26. Go to a lonely/deserted place; notice the hidden sounds there. Write about those sounds.

27. Read the warning label on a medicine. Write about taking care to avoid adverse reactions.

28. Count something. Write a poem celebrating the numbers.

October, Week Five

29. Write a vignette about your own life; go back at least a decade.

30. Use this line: *rain probably has no difficulty in falling.* (Richard Wilbur)

31. Write a poem of farewell, or an aubade.

Epilogue

Now you have reached the end of **my** discipline. What's next.

Do you think you have a new sense of discipline in your own writing? Are you going on from here? Do you need more prompts? Do you think you are ready to begin editing the poems you have written?

The answers to these questions I will leave up to you, dear writer. It is up to you now. You.

However, if you are wondering about my poems, the ones I wrote during my year of discipline, please look for the companion to this manual: *365 in the Rough: a year's adventure of poems,* coming soon.

Good luck!

As always, I wish you ... *good ink.*

CWB

Printed in the USA
CPSIA information can be obtained
at www.ICGtesting.com
LVHW031552310723
753891LV00009B/187

9 780359 565917